NEBO PETER C

THE
VIRGIN
MOST
POWERFUL

3 POWERFUL MARIAN DEVOTIONS THAT WILL CHANGE YOUR LIFE

The Virgin Most Powerful

3 Powerful Marian Devotions that will change your life

Copyright 2019 by Nebo Peter C

ISBN 978-978-975-650-6

Published by:

G-top Communications

Lagos, Nigeria

The Preface:

The history of mankind is a history of power, influence, and dominion. People have erected statutes, built structures in order to honor their gods, their goddesses, and their loved ones. In Indian culture, there are several structures and statues of different gods and goddesses; same in ancient Greek culture. In ancient Roman culture, the stories of Janus, Minerva, Juno, and several other Roman gods and goddesses have brought mankind to the understanding and perceptions of the ancient Romans in their interpretations of life and its meaning.

Definitely, I am not here to talk about statues, idolatry, cultures and traditions. I am here to preach Christ Jesus. I am here to talk about the great intercessory roles of his Mother Mary, the Virgin Most powerful, in the life of believers; that even though mankind has been besieged with stories of gods and goddesses, none of these stories is nowhere to be compared with the influence of Christ Jesus and His mother Mary in the history and total salvation of mankind for the past 2000 years ago.

For the past 2000 years ago, the power of Christ Jesus and His resurrection, who though he was God came to us in a manner we could reckon with, have continued to wield great influences among many nations. Christ has been taught and preached in many languages and in many dialects of the world. Men and women have received mighty healing in Jesus Christ. The lame had walked. The sick had become whole again. Miracles had been wrought and perfected in the name of Jesus. Universities, great citadels of learning, economies and many countries of the world have been established based on the principles taught by Jesus Christ and further elaborated by his disciples to the ends of the earth.

For once, O Christian Soul, I urge you to think about the influence of Christ Jesus, His teachings and His resurrection power which spread like wildfire when even the worship of Janus and other ancient Roman gods could not penetrate beyond the Indies. For once, think about the wide influence of Christianity brought to us by the fathers when the French Empire with its divine rights of kings could not last for more than 5 centuries. We say in our Igbo culture that, "he who has the knife and the yam dictates everything". Gamaliel told the people who were gathered in the Sanhedrin when the issues of Peter and other apostles were brought to him not to worry about these men of sublime and upright faith, but that if their cause were not ordained by God, their cause would die a natural death (Acts 5:34-40). So has it been with the powers and dictates of this world, but Christ Jesus has continued to reign for forever.

There is something then about Christ Jesus, the son of God, which ought to catch our spirit-soul and submerge them into meditational awakening. There is something about Jesus Christ that we ought to contemplate and elaborate. One of the many deeper revelations about Christ Jesus, as we say in our Igbo culture that one becomes good from within before it is expressed outside, is His mother Mary. Mary, the mother of Jesus, is an enigma. Mary, the mother of Jesus, is a deep mystery beyond comprehension. Mary, the mother of Jesus, is a deep revelation by God before the foundation of the world. We honor her as the mother of our Redeemer; we don't worship her.

THE INTRODUCTION:

At the wedding feast at Cana in Galilee, Mary, the mother of Jesus, instructed the disciples of Jesus to do whatever Jesus tells them to do (John2vs.5). At the skullcap hill of Golgotha, Jesus subdued in pains and agony commanded the disciple who stood by him to take Mary home as his mother (John 19:27). Between Mary's maternal instructions to the disciples at Cana in Galilee and Jesus patrimonial command to John, there exists a deep revelation between our Lord Jesus Christ and His Mother, Mary. Mary 'tells us to do'; and if we as Christ followers must do all that Jesus commanded us to do, then we must like John take Mary home as our mother.

At the cross, John represented us. At the cross, John represented the multitudes of men and women who would later come before the cross of Christ for the forgiveness of their sins and for the sanctification of their bodies. At this cross, amidst all the pains and the humiliations he suffered, Jesus equally 'commands' us to 'behold his mother'.

Definitely looking at the above biblical episodes, one would note that all these happened at the beginning of Jesus public ministry and at the end of his stay here on earth. One would also note that in all these magnanimous events Mary was deeply involved.

First, at the wedding feast at Cana in Galilee Mary urged the disciples to do whatever Jesus tells them to do (John 2vs.5). She interceded with Jesus as was against his time for public manifestation and had 6 empty jars of old wine ('oinos' in Greek) re-filled again with a new source of wine. Here, she was depicted as our 'Intercessor par excellence'; our Salvation Catalyst.

Second, at Golgotha, Mary stood vehemently by Jesus with the invisible swords of sorrows revealed by Simeon in Luke2 vs.35 piercing her heart as she watched her son died on that infamous gibbet. Here, she was revealed as the 'Mother of all sorrows; Queen of All hearts', who would rather stay besides us in moments of anguish than leave us. And unlike thieves and impostors, conmen and murderers, who according to the great historian

Cicero, would curse their mothers and spit on the faces of those who mock and execute them, Jesus squirmed in agony and tribulation on the cross uttered no condemnations. Jesus did not spit on the faces of those around. He was replete with forgiveness, peace and restoration. He gave us then his Mother to behold as our true maternal source of help and comfort; for He who had led us out of the dark ways of corruption ought to lead us, like a dying father about to bequeath his possessions to his children, into the new ways of "Being".

Interestingly then, it is imperative that one who must be a friend of Jesus must have an undeniable recourse to the person of Mary. It is imperative that one who must take Jesus as his Lord and personal savior must have a strong maternal recourse to his Mother. Mary's role in our redemption can never be denied. Mary's maternal succor in our quest to please God and attain His blessings can never be relegated.

In Rev.12 vs. 1, this passage written by John- the beloved apostle who took her home from the cross, Mary was revealed as the woman with a crown of 12 stars. '12' in ancient Judaic symbolism means 'a whole' or 'that which forms a whole'. We have the '12' tribes of Israel. We have the '12' apostles in the New Testament. '12' also represents the manifestation of the Trinity over the four corners of the world; for '3' multiplied by '4'equals to 12. Mary, being the Mother of God (Theotokos) and Queen of heaven, has maternal dominion over the four corners of the universe. The moon on her feet and the sun that made up her maternal garment indicate her resilient power and glory.

In Luke 1 vs. 39, she was revealed as the 'Help of Christians'. In Ezekiel 44 vs.2 and Luke 1 vs. 26-35, she was revealed as the 'Virgin most Powerful'. In Rev. 7 vs. 9, she was by inference revealed as the 'Queen of All Saints'; for what saints there are, apart from God, without her powerful intercession. In the Canticle of Canticles, the Songs of Solomon 7:5, she was revealed as the 'Tower of Ivory'. On the Pieta' and other artistic biblical representations of the Lamentations and Passions of Christ, she was revealed as the 'Refuge of sinners'; 'Comfort of the afflicted'.

The 'Pieta' is an inspired piece of art that depicts the Virgin Mary's cradling of Jesus at death. When the body of Jesus was brought down by Joseph of

Arimathea, he placed his body at the feet of Mary for consolation.

Verily, the Pieta has had a deep religious scar on my soul that the contours of these scars would remain forever indelible. While I was in my first year apostolic work (2002) as a senior Seminarian in Umuoji Anambra State, Nigeria, I met Sir Omenuko (Chief Lawrence Okeke), a blind rich man who was tremendously religious and had a special recourse to the Immaculate Heart of Mary. Sir Omenuko, prior to our meeting, was a reputed charismatic leader. He was a well-known philanthropist who encouraged economic dynamism but lost his two sights to river blindness years back.

One afternoon, I decided to visit him. It was around 12'O'clock in the afternoon. The beautiful expanse of Sir Omenuko's compound blossomed as I made my way to the living room adjacent his chapel. A lady in her late twenties came out and welcomed me. She went into the chapel and informed Sir Omenuko of my visit.

Calmly but with the lady's support, the old man wearied with age and blindness came out and joined me in the living room. I greeted him, introduced myself, and for minutes we had Father to son discussions. Of all that I discussed with Sir Omenuko, one discourse that struck the breastplate of my soul was his remarks on the Pieta'. He said and I re-quote:

"Upon all the blood stains, the open sores, his disfigured face, the wounds that deteriorated the body of Jesus at crucifixion, Mary did not mind the bruises of his stinking wounds. Mary did not consider his thick blood stains but cradled Jesus with great love and compassion. I want you to open your inner eyes and see the revelations of this great act. When the body of Jesus was brought down by Joseph of Arimathea and laid on her feet, Mary cradled the body of Jesus with love. What other mothers would find difficult to do, and even we - assuming we were told to cradle a dead body with such degree of wounds, Mary did with exceptional love.

Reflect on these my son. Know that no matter how stench a sinner's soul might smell; no matter how dirty his or her sinful garment is, Mary is ever ready to assist whoever comes to her seeking repentance and salvation through her son Jesus Christ. Mary is the maternal fear of the enemy. Mary will hug him, cradle her, and present them all before the cleansing fount of His sacrificial blood. Sincerely, in my years of wailing in solitude and in my blindness, I have never seen such a love so encompassing. Daily I draw my inner strengths from the sweet ocean of this love. My inner eyes have been opened to the mysteries thereof. How I wish my son you can activate the fiery darts of these mysterious revelations in your life for healing. Mary's acts and tender acts are mysteries beyond human explanations. They are mysterious as the deep blue sea and the child in the womb".

Oh, what a glorious recants!

But unfortunately, the person of Mary and her salvific role in our redemption have been subjects of intense discussions throughout the centuries. Maximalist tendencies and Minimalist approaches have emerged. Feminist and psychological interceptions have also risen in these regards.

Undoubtedly also, Mary's maternal role in assisting us to the throne of mercy and power has ruffled many feathers. It has chided many would-be Catholics. I'm not here to dispel the white soot of these doubts about Mary. I am not here to refute the necessary contingencies of these enormous spiritual controversies. St. Alphonsus Ligouri's book, the **Glories of Mary**, Mark Miravalle's book, **Introduction to Mary**, **Mary in the Catholic tradition** by Frederic M. Madonna, Pope John Paul II encyclical "**Redemptoris Mater**" and Rev. Fr. Gabriel Okeke's 22-paged discourse on "Hail Mary" are some books and discourses on Mary that might help an open-minded soul. What I'm here to do is simple: to hold you by the hands and present to you _3 powerful Marian devotions_ that influenced my life and that would change your life too. I presented these in ways so enriching and in a manner so simple.

Here also, I will briefly present to you 12 powerful Psalms for changing your life circumstances WITH PRAYER HINTS AND PARAPHRASES. These are the precinct of this book. These are the geographical portions of this work. And like St. Louis de Montfort said in his "Treatise on true Devotion to the Blessed Virgin" I conclude: God the Father gathered all the waters together and called them the seas. He gathered all his graces together and called them Mary" **(page 4, 'Treatise on True Devotion to the Blessed Virgin, 1987, Montfort Missionaries)**

CHAPTER 1

THE ROSARY- DEVOTION TO OUR LADY OF THE HOLY ROSARY

The Holy Rosary is one of the 3 Marian powerful devotions that would change your life for better. This is one of the three Marian devotions that has shattered the gates of hell and has freed many from the ravages of sin and death. This great Marian devotion has opened many doors. It has set a lot of prisoners free. Oh, through this devotion which is the most powerful of all Marian devotions, men have been raised from the pit of hell unto the plane of everlasting life. Women in their thousands have witnessed great divine turnarounds. Many impossible situations which hitherto seemed impossible had become possible. And in summing up these impossible possibilities of the Holy Rosary, Blessed Alan of the Rock had this to say:

'The Rosary shall be a powerful army against hell. It will destroy vice, decrease sin, and destroy heresies. It will cause good works to flourish; it will obtain for souls the abundant mercy of God; it will withdraw the hearts of men from the love of the world and its vanities, and will lift them to the desire of eternal things" *(Fifteen Promises of Mary, Our Lady's Rosary Makers of Australia, Inc.)*

THE HISTORY

Prior to the battle of Lepanto and in the year 1214, St. Dominic, according to Blessed Alan of the Rock, received the concept of the Holy Rosary in an apparition of the Blessed Virgin Mary. This apparition happened in the Church of Prouille 250 years before the birth of Blessed Alan. It became popular through the latter works of Blessed Alan and through other pious traditions. It was widely accepted in Europe until in the 17th Century when hagiographers like the Bollandists began to question its authenticity for lack of proper documentation.

But irrespective of the controversies shrouding the history of the Holy Rosary as given to St. Dominic and its later adjudication as a 'private revelation', the Holy rosary as a devotion to the Blessed Virgin Mary had become popular among the Catholics since the 13th Century. Numerous Popes, Saints and religious faithful have encouraged this wonderful devotion. Blessed Gimenez Malla is one saint to remember when we talk about this. Numerous Popes, saints and religious Faithful have gathered enough roses and had built wonderful beehives of spiritual strengths through the powers of this devotion and worthiness.

In the 16th Century, Pope Pius V included the Rosary as a major force in the General Roman calendar. This was after the victory at the Battle of Lepanto, when the Holy League formed by His Holiness and led by Don Juan de Austria destroyed the Turkish Ottoman Armada in the Gulf of Patras. This victory, according to pious tradition, was attributed to the intercessory role of the Blessed Virgin Mary, who on the eve of the battle was beseeched by Pope Pius V through a Rosary procession to intercede for the Holy Roman Catholic Empire. Thus, after the victory which witnessed miraculous turnarounds the Pope gave it the title "Feast of Our Lady of Victory", now "Our Lady of the Rosary" celebrated every October 7.

In the same vein, Pope Leo XIII called the "Rosary Pope" in his September 1 1883 encyclical, "Supremi apostolatus officio", instituted the month of October as a month of the Holy Rosary. The Pope urged for ***private and public recitation*** of the Holy Rosary. He issued 10 encyclicals and 5 apostolic letters on the Holy Rosary. He included the invocation "Queen of the Most Holy Rosary" to the

Litany of the Blessed Virgin Mary, called in another moniker, "the Litany of Loreto".

Blessed Alan of the Rock, the saint whose life had become synonymous with the revelations and promises of the Holy Rosary, wrote the '15 promises of the Holy Rosary'. The quote at the beginning of this chapter is one of the 15 sempiternal promises.

St. Louis de Montfort, a French Roman Catholic Priest and Confessor who died on April 28th 1716, 4 months before the Battle of Petrovaradin, composed a powerful masterpiece on the powers, miracles, and methods of praying the Rosary in His book, "Secret of the Rosary". His others works, the *'Secret of Mary"* and the *"True Devotion to Mary"*, influenced several Popes and had an exquisite impact on Pope John Paul II choice of "Totus tuus"- totally thine- as his Apostolic motto. In his encyclical *"Redemptoris Mater"*, Pope John Paul II, who was canonized as Saint John Paul II on April 27th 2014, commended St. Louis de Montfort for his efforts in Mariology. He called him one of the early writers and witnesses of Marian Spirituality. In his encyclical, *"Rosarium Virginis Mariae"*, the Holy pontiff identified the Rosary as a contemplative prayer that leads us to Jesus

through Mary. He added the "Mysteries of Light'
into the cycle of the mysteries of Christ that are to
be contemplated while praying the Holy Rosary.
Like St. Pius X in his encyclical "***Ad diem illium***" and
St. Pius V in his papal bull "***Consueverunt***", St. John
Paul II wrote in ***Rosarium Virginis Mariae***:

*"The Rosary, though clearly Marian in character, is
at heart a Christocentric prayer. In the sobriety of
its elements, it has all the depth of the Gospel
message in its entirety, of which it can be said to be
a compendium. ...Through the Rosary the faithful
receive abundant grace, as though from the very
hands of the Mother of the Redeemer"*.

Consequently, the devotion to Mary through the
Rosary took another twist by the middle of 19th
century to the beginning of 20th Century. The
Marian apparitions in Lourdes in which St.
Bernadette saw the Blessed Virgin Mary dressed in
white with a golden rosary in her hands, and the
Marian apparitions in Fatima in which Blessed Lucy,
St. Jacinta Marto and St. Francisco Marto were
urged to pray the Rosary daily brought new
resurgence in the recitation and praying of the Holy
Rosary. With these apparitions, the movements
that followed and the torchlights that were lighted

gave rise to many Marian devotions through the Rosary. Many Marian institutions sprung up. Many Cathedrals, homes and shrines were dedicated to Our Lady of the Holy Rosary. Many Marian Confraternities arose and the consecration to the Immaculate Heart of Mary became much popular.

WHAT IS THE ROSARY

The Rosary, meaning in Latin-"Rosarium"-a garland of roses, is a string of beads containing sets of ten Hail Mary's with a crucifix and set of three Hail Mary's at the beginning. Each of these sets of ten Hail Mary's called a decade, (5 decade in all and 20 decades when all the 4 mysteries of Christ are said and contemplated), is preceded by "Our Father", "Glory be.." and a particular mystery of Christ's manifestation. With the prayers we contemplate and meditate the joyful mysteries of Christ, his sorrowful mysteries, his glorious mysteries and the mysteries of his light.

The Holy Rosary according to pious tradition was predicated on the 150 numbers of the Book of Psalms. With this artful and masterful divine connectivity, the Catholics especially the Dominicans prayed and beseeched the Mother of

God for her help and intercession with prayers, meditations, Litany of the Blessed Virgin Mary and beautiful Marian hymns.

On October 16th 2002, Pope John Paul II changed the number of the Hail Mary's to be said in total while praying the Rosary from 150 to 200, when he added the 'Mysteries of Light' into cycle of the mysteries that are to be contemplated while praying the Rosary. By adding the mysteries of Light, the Pope made the Rosary 20 decades in all instead of the 15 previous decades. With this celebrated supreme Pontification, the Joyful mystery is now said on Mondays and Saturdays (Lenten periods exclusive), the Sorrowful mystery on Tuesdays and Fridays, the Glorious mystery on Wednesdays and Sundays, the mystery of Light on Thursdays, while a pious soul charged with the love of God and led by a specific intention can decide to contemplate and pray the full mysteries in a day.

HOW TO SAY OR RECITE THE ROSARY EFFECTIVELY

"And I felt his voice take the sword out of my hand"….Charles Heston (Ben Hur)

During our short stay in St. Pius X Spiritual Seminary Akwukwu, there was one epic historical film amongst others that rented our recreational space. It was "***Ben Hur***" by Metro-Goldwyn- Mayer. '***Ben Hur***' by Metro-Goldwyn-Mayer was a 1959 remake of the 1925 earlier version. They were adapted from the novel, "Ben Hur: A Tale of Christ", written by General Lew Wallace in 1880.

 In this 1959 adaptation, Charlton Heston known as Ben Hur was a wealthy Jewish prince. He was framed up by his friend Messala, a Roman Consul, during the arrival of Valerius Gratus, a Roman Prefect and Governor, into Judaea. Ben Hur was later convicted to suffer as a galley slave. His mother, Miriam, and his Sister, Tirzah, were also condemned to suffer his fate. They were sent to Rome as prisoners.

While in the prison, Miriam and Tirzah contacted a deadly leprosy. They suffered hate and indignation and were later driven away from the city into a protracted valley of Lepers.

But of all the twists and turns, the Chariot race and the Jesus's acts and utterances that made Ben Hur an epic historical film, one particular intermediate scene that made us trembled with passion and got our feet stuck to the ground as if glued with cohesive was the scene of Jesus death on the cross; when his precious blood, flushed down by a heavy rainstorm, touched the bodies of Miriam and Tirzah and healed them of their leprosies. This scene of all the dramas that happened got us, especially me, intoxicated with tears of joy.

ON THE HOLY ROSARY,

One of the essential weapons of exorcising our minds of the evils of corruption and healing our spirit- soul of the leprosies of sins that morally pollute our world is the Holy Rosary. The Holy Rosary is a massive weapon of grace and exorcism. The Rosary is a massive weapon of sempiternal grace. It draws from the heart and reaches to the inner soul. Like the raindrops of blood that touched Miriam and Tirzah and healed them of their leprosies, and like the sweet amazing voice of Jesus that beckoned Ben Hur to drop the sword off his hands, such are the huge benefits of the Holy Rosary on those who recite it daily and meditate contemplatively on the mysteries of the Redeemer that wrought our salvation. The Rosary according to Fr. Michael Barone is a powerful armor of God. In them, we open ourselves to divine touch of healing and redemption. In them, we hear Jesus speak to us as through his mother. And to the extent we revel on this divine touch and hear the sweet amazing voice of Jesus to that extent we are constantly freed from leprosies of pride, malice, fear, fornication, and other evil vices that bedevil our world.

HOW THEN DO YOU, O CHRISTIAN SOUL, SAY THE HOLY ROSARY AND USURP THE MANY PROMISES THEREIN?

First, my candid advice to you, O Christian soul, that wants to enjoy the qualitative promises of the Holy Rosary is to read the ominous work of St. Louis de Montfort on the "Secret of the Rosary". There as through the window you will observe the countenances, the responses, the miracles and the reflections that informed the recitations of the Holy Rosary.

Secondly, throughout the years I was consecrated to the Immaculate Heart of Mary up till now, I have adjudged meditation and contemplation the best ways to enjoy and obtain the promises of the Rosary. The 7 spiritual nuggets below, as in the "Complete" biblical sense of the number '7', are my contemplative inclinations. The 7 spiritual nuggets below, as in the extended miraculous sense of the number '7', are my superlative inspirations dawned with the Excellency of the Holy Ghost in reciting and praying the Rosary. So when you pray the Rosary, O Christian soul, do well like in other Catholic prayer books and penitential rites to have them in mind.

SPIRITUAL NUGGET 1

The rosary is an intercessory and contemplative prayer. It is an intercessory prayer that leads us to Jesus through Mary. In them, we gather the graces of God as the waters cover the sea.

SPIRITUAL NUGGET 2

 When you begin the Holy Rosary, make the Sign of the cross and start with the invocation to the Holy Ghost. The Holy Ghost is the giver of life. The Holy Ghost is the re-newer of minds. No biblical revelations, wonders and prophetic ceremonious feats had been recorded in history without the influence of the Holy Ghost. Simeon was filled with the Holy Ghost when he met the child Jesus (Luke 2:25-26). Jesus left Galilee into the wilderness and was filled with the Holy Ghost. Saying the Rosary, you are about to experience the love and grace of God made manifest in Jesus through her mother, so the Holy Ghost being the third person of the Trinity prepares your mind, body and soul for this awesome experience.

Secondly, by inviting the Holy Ghost to come down upon you, you invite Him to dispel every form of darkness around you. You invite Him to renew you as it was in the beginning of creation when the whole earth was without form and darkness upon the surface of the earth. You invite Him to fill your mind with power and your spirit with understanding as it were in the days of Pentecost when the apostles charged by the Holy Ghost came out with power and boldness. Bear in mind then that the Holy Ghost is not a thing or a past experience as most Christians view Him. The Holy Ghost is still a living experience and the third Person of the Trinity. He is a person, not a thing; power and authority beyond measure. Therefore, you must desire Him daily and in the recitation of the Holy Rosary and as the Psalmist had said in Psalm 63:1: **"O God, you are my God, and I long for you. My whole being desires you; like a dry, worn-out, and waterless land..."**

SPIRITUAL NUGGET 3

After the invitation of the Holy Ghost, next is the Creed. The Creed is the Roman Catholic article of Faith. It is condensed into two gravitational poles: the Trinitarian belief and the Catholic beliefs. The creed is the basis of the Catholic faith. It was formed in AD 325 in the city of Nicaea and adopted to debunk Arian claims that Jesus was no God. So when you recite this article of Faith, recite with it the "*Homoousios*" (of one substance with God) nature of Christ in mind. Recite it with uttermost devotion. Recite the creed calling to mind the Catholic beliefs in God the Father, the creator; God the son, the Redeemer; God the Spirit, the advocate, the Holy Catholic church, the communion of Saints, the resurrection of the body and life everlasting.

SPIRITUAL NUGGET 4

'Our Father" follows after the Creed. Our Father is the Lord's Prayer that Jesus taught us when the apostles asked him: Lord, teach us how to pray (Luke 11:1-4)? This is a prayer of glory, power and total submission. With this powerful prayer of the Lord's command, Jesus laid down for us 'blueprints and eternal sequence' by which we ought to pray and approach God Our Father:

- ✓ First, by acknowledging His authority over all things; His authority over the deep and His authority over the heavens,

- ✓ Second, by giving Him honor and glory due His Name,

- ✓ Third by confessing our sins,

- ✓ Fourth, by asking for unlimited supply of our daily earthly and spiritual needs; bearing in mind that whatever good we desire of God is to be used for the good of all, not to be taking alone. This is the essence of God's kingdom here on earth.

- ✓ And fifth, by seeking for His divine protection always....

So when you O Christian soul recite this wonderful prayer of the Lord's command, do with it hunger, desire and vision of the Fatherhood of God, Our Creator.

Again, one beautiful thing with "Our Father' is that it coincides with Psalm 91 and with the Hebrew's notions of "El-yon", "El-shadai" and "Yahweh". God is our ultimate help in times of need. Exodus 15 vs. 11 says, 'Lord, who among the gods is like you. Who is like you, wonderful in holiness, who can work miracles and mighty acts like yours"? Job 33:4 says, "God was the spirit that made me; El-Shaddai the breath that gave me life". Psalm 37:5 says, "Commit your destiny to Yahweh, be confident in Him, and He will act". Proverb 18:10 says, "The name of Yahweh is a strong tower; the upright runs to it and is secure". Thus, by saying "Our Father" with vision and power, O Christian soul, and meditating on these scriptural wonders through which God, Our Father, had made name for himself, you commit your body, your soul, your mind to God as in the Hebrew's explication of the word "**Shamah**". You re-enact once again the Authority of God over all things. You confess your dependency on God and your beliefs in the power of the Almighty to make crooked lines straight.

SPIRITUAL NUGGET 5

The Hail Mary's…

Hail Mary is Angel Gabriel's greetings to Mary in Luke 1 vs. 28. In one part, it is suffused with

Elizabeth's greetings to Mary in Luke 1 vs. 42, and in the other part, it is excellently garnished with the Church's requests to Mary, the mother of God, for her powerful intercession as we witnessed in John 2: 3-5.

Now when you recite these Angelic-divine greetings to Mary together with the church's glorious intentions, meditate solemnly on the spiritual meanings of these greetings and intentions-which Father Gab Okeke had put together in his wonderful discourse on "Hail Mary". Envision the Mother of God before you while you pray and decorate her victorious feet and perpetual crown (Rev 12:1) with the rose flowers of your Holy Rosary. Remember that the Rosary means in Latin **"*Rosarium*"**- a garland of roses, and that in some quarters and cultures it is believed that the best expression of love and honor you can give to someone is the one done with gifts of flowers. Mary is a perfect example of love, grace, purity, meekness, humility and obedience. She deserves our honor and homage. Oh! Mary had opened the gates of total reconciliation and forbearance for us, whilst Eve, the first woman, had caused us by their disobedience, death, misfortunes and ancient gates of afflictions. Mary, the mother of Jesus, leads us constantly to the throne of grace and mercy, to the throne of greatness and everlasting happiness; whereas Eve, the first woman, had by their disobedience led us out of the ancient thrones of the Paradise.

Again, when you recite or say the Hail Mary's meditatively, do it with consciousness and with every sense of honor. You are not worshipping Mary by saying the Holy Rosary; rather you are giving her the honor due to her as the mother of God and asking for her glorious intercessions. You are giving her the *'Hyperdulia'* of her eternal beauty which Angel Gabriel replicated in Luke 1 vs. 28. You are giving her the honor due her perpetual divine excellence. And no man of meritorious size and consciousness, I believe, would ever neglect the care and promptness of a good mother talk less of Jesus when he sees us honor her mother. I repeat again, that no man of external influence would ever disrespect the remembrance and memorial of a loving mother. History is replete with men and women who have done such honors and have even erected statues in order to celebrate and remember their mothers. As I write this, plans are underway in Kensington Palace Wales of Prince William and Prince Harry planning to erect a monumental statue in honor and remembrance of their late mother, Princess Diana, who died in a car crash 20 years ago. The late Princess touched so many lives and according to her sons' narratives: "it is now appropriate to recognize her positive impact at home and abroad with the monument. We hope the statue will help all those who visit Kensington Palace to reflect on her life and legacy"- Culled from **"The guardian" UK Newspaper, 28th January 2017**.

Now if men and women of high esteem know how to perform and do remembrance deeds for their late mothers, what of we who have been brought into the son-ship of God through Jesus and her mother Mary. Therefore, when you recite the Holy Rosary meditatively and decorate the victorious feet and crown of the Blessed Virgin Mary with the rose flowers of your rosary, you portray in deep magnitude the signs of this love and glorious affection.

SPIRITUAL NUGGET 6

On 'Glory be to the Father" and the Mysteries of Christ

The mysteries of Christ are the cornerstones of the Rosary. They are reasons we also recite and pray the Rosary.

Concomitantly, these mysteries follow immediately after the 'Glory-be' and short prayers for our departed brethren, especially those in purgatory, have been said.

And what are these mysteries of Christ?

These mysteries of Christ are the four cardinal phases that marked the historical existence of Christ. They are the ***Joyful mysteries***-encapsulated in the Virgin Mary's Fiat to the Angel, her maternal visitation to Elizabeth in Luke1 vs.39-45, Christ birth, His presentation at the Temple and his instructions to the elders. They are the ***Sorrowful mysteries***-encapsulated in Jesus prayer and agony in the garden, His scourging at the pillar, his crowning with thorns, His carrying of the Cross and his death on the cross. They are the ***Mysteries of Light***- encapsulated in the Baptism of Christ, the wedding feast at Cana, the proclamation of the kingdom of God, the transfiguration and the institution of the Holy Eucharist. They are the ***Glorious mysteries***- encapsulated in Christ's resurrection from the dead, His ascension into Heaven, the descent of the Holy Ghost, the

Assumption of Mary and her glorious coronation as the Queen of Heaven and earth.

Each of these mysteries contains gems of spiritual energies and fortifications. Each of these mysteries contains gems of supernatural enlightenment. In overall, they are the organogram of the mysteries that wrought our salvation.

So when you, O Christian soul, comes at the end of each decade of the Rosary and is time to say and contemplate the mysteries of Christ, do it with the vision of the Holy Ghost, whose job also is to present to you in pictures what you see and read in the scriptures, and mull over contemplatively on the mysteries of our Redeemer.

See yourself helping Jesus carry His Cross (Sorrowful mysteries). See yourself in the same temple with the child Jesus where he lays bare the foundational truths of life and eternity before you (joyful mysteries). See yourself in the midst of the apostles when the Holy Ghost descended upon them and charged them with power and innermost revelations (Glorious mysteries). See yourself at the transfiguration where Jesus surrounded by Moses and Elijah revealed to Peter, James and John the secrets of the Kingdom (Mysteries of the Light). See yourself participating in these mysteries and say a powerful, short and distinct prayer at the end of each mystery.

For instance, if after contemplating on the crucifixion of Jesus or his first miracle at Cana in Galilee, or the Virgin Mary's visit to Elizabeth, or the resurrection of Jesus, you can say any short prayers of YOUR CHOICE respectively, with power and faith, after each mystery. This is where the intercessional power and force of the Rosary comes in. For instance, I can pray according the mysteries mentioned above:

Every chain of confusion assigned to my destiny is broken in the name of Jesus.

Every sickness, spiritual blindness racketeering my physical and spiritual progress be nailed permanently to the cross of Christ.

Through thy wounds O Jesus, thy name which is above every name, heal me from the ravages of sin and death (For the crucifixion of Jesus on the cross)

Or........

O Lord, through this miracle of turning water into wine make my life full of your miracles in Jesus name

O Lord, you turned water into wine, turn around all my difficulties or our difficulties in Jesus name

(For the first miracle at Cana in Galilee)

Or........

O Mary, conceived without sin, teach me Humility and come to my aid

O Mary, mother of the Redeemer, you visited Elizabeth and showed her love and care, teach me how to please God in all things and intercede for me, O Mary.

(For the visitation of Elizabeth)

Or........

O Lord, by the power of thy resurrection, drive away every old enemy of sin and corruption in me! Cast into fire every ancient costume of wickedness and destroy every vengeful incantation. Let thy

power of resurrection be in me always. Surround
me with thy power and guide me always.

(For the resurrection of Christ)

Say these prayers with faith, knowing that that
which you ask for shall be granted unto you. And as
they are in these short distinct prayers, you can
form other intentions of your needs or THOSE OF
OTHERS and attach them to these mysteries of our
salvation.

Again O Christian soul, the reasons why we
contemplate the mysteries and attach a specific
intention or intentions to them are to teach you
humility, purpose (James 4:3) and dependency on
God. As kids we believed in miracles. As kids we
believed that nothing is impossible which we ask
for. But as adults, our thoughts and beliefs as kids
tend to give way because we started to focus more
on our problems instead on God. Like Peter, we
tend to focus more on the vast storms of our life,
the bills we have to pay et cetera, instead on Jesus,
the author and Finisher of our Faith; as a child will
always look toward his parents and a maiden unto

her mistress. Like Ishmael, we labor ostensibly in the flesh than in the Spirit like Jacob; for Zechariah 4:14 says, "It is neither by might nor by power, says Yahweh Sabaoth, but by the spirit". This is in retrospect to the Abrahamic kind of faith which by extension we are all called in to partake; so that in blessings we shall all be blessed, and in multiplying we shall also multiply.

Therefore O Christian soul, by contemplating the mysteries of Christ and attaching specific intentions to them, ***we also remind ourselves that the lives we live and enjoy are mysteries; that no human intelligence would explain better the complete mysteries of our lives than when we focus on Jesus and participate actively in his mysteries***. John 1:1-4 says that, "In the beginning was the Word; the Word was with God and the Word was God (Jesus).... Through Him all things came into being, not one thing came into being except through Him".

Also by contemplating the mysteries of Christ and attaching specific intentions to them, we recall in us that initial mind of 'GOD' and total dependency on Him. Not that we are called not to partake in any given work or labor but that our works and labor should be made perfect through our trust and dependency on God. Furthermore O Christian soul, by contemplating the mysteries of Christ and attaching specific intentions to them, we recall through Virgin Mary that it is the Lord who gives us the power to get wealth; that it is in laboring more in the spirit than in the flesh that the mysteries of our lives are gradually revealed to us, and that it is in saying 'Fiat" to those things which have been revealed to us through our Lord Jesus Christ that the seeds and fruits of his incarnate wisdom are born in us.

SPIRITUAL NUGGET 7

On the "Hail Holy Queen and the Litany of Loreto"

One of the many Marian hymns and prayers that I enjoy singing or praying at the end of the Rosary is the "Hail Holy Queen". The Hail Holy Queen, in Latin "Salve Regina", is a Marian hymn/prayer poised with enormous supplications. It is said at the end of the Rosary. In its Latin original form, which is the "Salve Regina", it is sung in some quarters at the close of Compline. In its Latin original form, which is the "Salve Regina", it is sung in some quarters by decedent's fellow priests at the end of a priest funeral. The Cistercians sing it daily as part of their processional hymns. The Sailors are in deep love with this Marian hymn. According to Fr. Juniper Carol, sailors had chosen this hymn as part of the ritual for the blessing of a ship.

The hail Holy Queen is a powerful Marian prayer. It is a prayer of special request beseeching the Mother of God to come to our aid and save us from the perils, tribulations, and vicissitudes of this life. No other Marian hymn has had more appeal to me than this glorious hymn. So when you sing this glorious hymn or recite it, O Christian Soul, beseech the Mother of God through her powerful intercessions to save you from perils and tribulation of this world. Make unequivocal demands to her that heaven is your target. Remind her with this glorious hymn all that you have asked for and prayed for in the preceding chaplets of the Holy Rosary, and for her to present them all before the THRONE OF GRACE and MERCY. St. Bonaventure said and I interpret, "no creature can help us better than Mary". No one can suffice to intercede for us better than Mary.

On the other hand, the Litany of the Blessed Virgin called in another moniker, the Litany of Loreto, is a compendium of all the Marian titles used both formally and informally for the Blessed Virgin Mary. They are often recited "as a call and response chant in group settings"-Wikipedia.org.

 Being a unique compendium of the titles and names addressed to the Virgin Mary, the Litany of Loreto is said immediately after the Hail Holy Queen. They are more than 20 titles given to Mary. The beauty of this litany is that each of these titles has biblical reference.

IN CONCLUSION

My beloved and dear Christian Soul, whose only spiritual aspirations have been those of the Father through Jesus and Mary, the reflections and spiritual nuggets above on reciting the Holy Rosary are my private reflections and deep spiritual introspections on saying and reciting the Holy Rosary. As you can see, not all the prayers and meditations of the Holy Rosary were fully discussed here but reflections were made on those prayers and meditations which are the hallmarks of the Holy Rosary. Take these as my jute bags of inspirations in helping you pray the Rosary effectively. Please do reflect also on other historical and ascetical writings on the Holy Rosary, especially the ones that have Pontifical approbations. May the Lord of Hosts bless you and guide you always. Amen!

CHAPTER TWO

DEVOTION TO OUR LADY OF PERPETUAL HELP

In Genesis 2:18, God said, "It is not good for man to be alone. I will make for him a suitable helper". God then caused Adam to sleep and in his sleep He formed Eve.

 Eve, through the instrumentality of the devil, became the first woman through which sin and death entered into world. Mary the mother Of Jesus on the other hand, through her willful obedience and submission to the Almighty, became the second woman and that singular vessel of honor through which salvation and perpetual grace have entered into the world again.

Definitely, these stories of creation and re-creation, of Adam and Eve, of Jesus and our mother Mary, are ones we must take with utmost reverence and deeper understanding. They remind us of God's undeniable love in the affairs of men (Hebrew 1:1-2). They remind us how throughout the ages God had sent prophets, priests and Kings to call His people back to Himself, and in the last days sent His only begotten son, Jesus Christ, through the instrumentality of the Virgin Mary to save us and redeem us from the ravages of sin and death. They are equally ones that remind us _that in all things we need divine help and assistance_; that in all things and at all times we cannot do without God, for cut off from GOD we can do nothing (John 15:5).

Surely, this divine call for help is equally replicated in our daily lives and activities. From childhood to adulthood, we need others to grow, to explore, to become and to actualize our dreams. We cannot do it alone. You cannot do it alone. I cannot do it alone. People, in whatever form and dimension, had played significant roles in our lives. People, in whatever form and dimension, had rendered significant helps in who we become and in what we do. Thus, 1 plus 1 in human calculations means 2, but in the heavenly calculations and assignments, 1 plus 1 might mean another significant number.

Now, one of the heavenly divine calculations of divine powerful assistance through which men and women have received untold helps is the devotion to OUR LADY OF PERPETUAL HELP.

The devotion to Our Lady of Perpetual help is one of the many Marian devotions which have caused men to turn back from pit of destruction. Women have received inestimable helps and miraculous interventions through this devotion. It is one of the giants in Marian devotions. And if the testimonies of this gracious devotion would be recorded in one book, the pages of this new book cannot contain all that would be recorded of this gracious Marian devotion.

Of records, many have testified miraculous helps doing this devotion. Many have posited untold and mighty turnarounds doing this wonderful devotion to Our Lady of Perpetual Help through which we seek Mary's perpetual divine intercession. The good thing about this devotion and about its outward impacts is that I have seen aircrafts, Churches, cities and ships named after Our Lady of Perpetual Help. The Republic of Haiti has Our Lady of Perpetual Help as her Patroness. The municipal of Almoradi in Spain has Our Lady of Perpetual Help as her Patroness too.

THE ORIGIN

Historically, the devotion to Our Lady of Perpetual, or expressed in similar fashion "Our Mother of Perpetual Help", started in the 15th Century AD. It started with a celebrated and reported Byzantine image of the Blessed Virgin Mary. In this Holy

Image, Mary, the Mother of God, was captured wearing a dress of dark red with a blue mantle that connotes her perpetual virginity and a veiled cloak that connotes her pure modesty. She was carrying our Lord Jesus Christ. On the two sides of this venerated image stand Archangel Michael and Archangel Gabriel with Mary looking towards us, the faithful, and pointing at her son, our Lord Jesus Christ, as our true Savior. To the left side of this glorious image is Archangel Michael holding the spear, the wine-soaked sponge and the crown of thorns. To the right side of this powerful Icon is Archangel Gabriel holding the cross and the nails. These are and were the very instruments with which our Lord Jesus Christ was condemned to death. They are also the very instruments of his triumphant victory as the golden background of this venerated image signifies Christ the Victorious who is sited at the right hand of God in heaven. On the Virgin Mary's forehead is the star of heaven. This star connotes the Mother of God as the Star of the Sea also.

Truly, this venerated IMAGE or Holy Icon explains that Mary is our *"**Hodighitria"*** in Greek, meaning- the one who guides us to the Redeemer.

The image depicts also the Virgin Mary's readiness at all times, just like in the Pieta, to assist us in every difficult situation and temptation when we call upon her intercessory help.

On this venerated image, we see the child Jesus lose one of his sandals in trepidation seeing the instruments of his passion but grasps the hand of his mother in comfort; a deep sign of affection and portrayal that Mary is Larger than life; a deep sign that Mary is our "Hodighitria".

On the background behind the image, we see blessedness; we see sanctity. Every Holy image conveys deep spiritual meaning. Prophets, Kings, Priests, often fast to receive divine inspiration and revelations. So on the venerated image, Mary gives us the hope that Jesus is our Redeemer. On this venerated image, Jesus looks at his mother Mary and points to her as our "Perpetual help and 'Hodighitria' in times of trepidations and dangers. On this venerated image also, thousands of souls have converged here over the centuries to receive hope and miracles from this venerated image like from the fountain.

POWERS AND MIRACLES

On the Powers and miracles of this Holy Icon of the Mother of God, which some pious tradition believed was drawn by St. Luke the apostle, it started in the 15th century. It started in the Island of Crete when a certain merchant acquired the Holy Icon and began to sail to Rome with it. On his way, a terrible storm arose and threatened the lives of those in the ship. Seeing that their lives were in danger, the merchant with other passengers sought the intercessory help of the Blessed Virgin Mary. The storm stopped. The ship became normal, and they reached their destination in peace.

While in Rome, this merchant stayed in the house of a friend who harbored him until he became sick and was dying. On his death bed, the merchant entrusted the Holy icon to his friend. He pleaded that the Holy Icon be put up for public veneration. His friend didn't do as he was told. He was rather convinced by his wife to keep the Holy image for their personal use. Several divine warnings followed this obstinacy through dreams and manifestations until the man died having failed to put up the Holy Image for public veneration. After his death, his daughter also had a dream in which our Blessed mother requested that the Holy icon should be venerated between the Basilicas of St. Mary Major and St. John the Lateran in Rome. After much pleas and miraculous manifestations, the Holy icon was consequently transferred from the merchant's house to the Church of St. Mathew.

For the next 300 years, the Holy Icon was housed in the Church of St. Mathew, between the Basilicas of St. Mary Major and St. John the Lateran. Great graces were bestowed upon the faithful. Many pilgrims flocked to the Church of St. Mathew Via Merulana to venerate the HOLY Icon and receive graces. Miracles flowed. Many astounding testimonies were heard of these glorious visits. One of such glorious testimonies was a paralyzed man, who on the day the Holy Icon was transferred from the merchant's house to the Church of St. Mathew, was cured of his paralysis instantly.

Then in 1798, Napoleon troops, during the fifth coalition of the West against Napoleon, invaded the Church of St. Mathew and destroyed it. They took captive of the church and brought it down.

But the Holy Icon was miraculously rescued by some Augustinian friars who were in charge of the church. They took it and transferred it to the Church of St. Mary Major in Posterula (an Augustinian Church) where it was neglected and forgotten for another 40 years.

For another 40 years, the Holy Icon was forgotten in St. Mary's church in Posterula. It was rediscovered again through divine and miraculous intervention. It was rediscovered after Fr. Marchi and Fr. Francis Blosi of the blessed memory wrote wonderful testimonies about the Holy Icon and of the Blessed Virgin Mary's desires for the Holy Icon to be honored between the Basilicas of St. Mary Major and St. John Lateran.

Thus in December 1865, Fr. Nicolas Mauron, the Redemptorists Superior General then, sought an audience with Pope Pius IX. He presented Fr. Marchi's revelations about the Holy Icon to the Holy See, who as a little Redemptorists' student witnessed the Holy Icon. He also presented Fr. Blosi's request of the Blessed Virgin Mary, that the Holy Icon should be honored between St. Mary's

Major and St. John Lateran. The Pope under the anointing of his apostolic virtues told Fr. Mauron "to make her known throughout the world". He wrote to the Cardinal Prefect of the Holy See. He ordered that the Holy Icon be entrusted to the Redemptorists by the Augustinians, and for the Holy Icon to be honored in the Church of St. Alphonsus. The Redemptorists had in their search for a befitting place to build a Church for public veneration built the Church of St. Alphonsus down the street from St. Mary's Major. The site of the Church of St. Alphonsus was the same site the Church of St. Mathew was built and where the Holy Icon was once venerated before the church was destroyed by Napoleon troops led by Louis-Alexandrie Berthier.

In 1855, the Redemptorists had purchased the Villa Caserta in Rome along Via Merulana, but unknown to them this was once the Church of St. Mathew and the site which the Blessed Virgin Mary chose as the Icon's shrine. This divine connectivity necessitated Pope Pius IX request for the Holy Icon to be transferred to the Church of St. Alphonsus and to be venerated there again, and for the Redemptorists, who later took possession of the

Holy icon, to supply another picture of Our Lady of Perpetual Help to the Augustinians in exchange for their goodwill.

Till this day, the Holy Icon of Our lady of Perpetual Help has been under the custody of the Redemptorists in Rome, who are also in charge of other Marian religious works of arts, with many copies and many representations of this holy image in different churches and homes.

THE MIRACLES

One of the miracles that became popular after Pope Pius IX had entrusted the Miraculous Image to the Redemptorists was in 1866. It was about a little boy of four who was terribly sick and dying. This little boy could be likened to Lucas Batista Maeda de Mourao, the ten years old Brazilian boy who was healed of brain damage through the miraculous intercessions of St. Francisco Marto and St. Jacinta Marto.

On the boy's case, the doctors had given up. They had diagnosed his case as helpless and hopeless. No amount of hope seemed to come by. But the mother of the boy was hopeful and believing God for a miracle. Thus on the day the Holy Icon was to be transferred officially to the Church of St. Alphonsus, the mother of the sick boy brought him onto an open window when she heard the chants of the processional hymns. As the procession progressed near her house, she looked prayerfully at the Holy Icon and prayed deeply: "Dear blessed mother, either cure my boy or take him to paradise!"

Our Blessed Mother chose the first and the boy was cured at once. The next day, the boy with her mother went to the Church of St. Alphonsus and standing in front of the miraculous image and Holy Icon, the little boy waved his little hands to Our Mother of Perpetual Help and said "grazie, grazie"...thank you, thank you.

Another important miracle of heavy spiritual relevance was the healing of Jose Carlos, son of Marquis of Rioflorido, from pleurisy. This happened in Almoradi, Spain, in the year 1918. Carlos's mother, the noble Lady Desamparado Fontes, had touched a silk cloth to the Icon of Our Lady of Perpetual Help in Rome. When she came back, she fed her son with the silk cloth. Her son was completely cured of the respiratory problem he had after he was fed with the silk cloth. This story became popular in Almoradi, Spain, that in 1945 Pope Pius XII declared Our Lady of Perpetual Help Patroness of Almoradi (culled from newyorklatinculture.com).

The same Pope Pius XII in 1942 declared Our Lady of Perpetual Help Patroness of Haiti, after the Haitians had credited the miraculous end to a cholera and smallpox outbreak in 1882 to Our Lady of Perpetual Help. This was 8 years before Pope Pius XII promulgated the Assumption of the Blessed Virgin Mary ex-cathedra in his apostolic constitution, "Munificentissimus Deus".

THE NOVENA BOOKLET AND THE BACLARAN MIRACLES

There are many miracles associated with our Lady's Holy icon. It will be worthy to note that most of these miracles are individual experiences. The novena to Our Lady of Perpetual Help booklet is full of these individual testimonies. Between 1871 and 1891 alone in the United States, there were about 387 recorded miracles of such individual testimonies.

 The Baclaran shrine in Manila Bay Philippines is one outstanding Marian shrine in the world dedicated to Our Lady of Perpetual Help. It is called a shrine of miracles. It is called the national shrine of Our Mother of Perpetual Help; a shrine of solace; SANCTUARY FOR ALL. Its entrance has more than 50 doors and its missionary activities play out 24/7. Take time, O Christian soul, to visit this shrine or hear the testimonies that emanate from the conclave of this shrine in honor of Our Lady of Perpetual Help. You can become part of these testimonies by joining their online prayer requests or by supporting the shrine through one of her charitable works of reconciliation called the **_SEVEN PILLARS_**.

The Baclaran SHRINE, since her official establishment in December 5 1958, has recorded over 300,000 miracles. Each of these miracles is defined according to <u>17 Classes of favors</u>; from Spiritual Favors, Conversion, Peace in the Home, Reconciliation, Partner in Life, Health and Recovery from Sickness, Delivered from All Dangers, Gift of a Child and Safe Delivery, Financial Help, Education and Success in Studies Board Exam, Travel Abroad, Local Employment, Overseas Employment, Social Justice and Peace in Society, Legal Favors, Temporal Favors to blessings and favors classified as unspecified.

Right now, one of the famous TESTIMONIES of the Baclaran Marian shrine was a woman whose son was a drug addict. The stories of drugs addicts have always been stories of treacherous grips and gut wrenching paths. It was equally same with this woman's son. His son was married and had two children under his care. Each time the son got high on drugs, he would come back home threatening to kill the mother and everyone. This became serious worries for the mother who was a true devotee to Our Lady of Perpetual Help. The mother would pray day and night for her son like St. Monica did for St. Augustine. For four years, she was always praying for her son and asking for the great intercessions of Our Lady of Perpetual Help. Eventually, her prayers were answered. Her son became freed from drug addiction. He found a job in a shipping company abroad and dedicated his life to prayer and hard work.

Like this woman's personified encounter and blessings also, every year in Baclaran shrine, every month in Baclaran shrine, there are always testimonies and favors of one answered prayer or another. The latest in the dominion of these testimonies is that Baclaran Shrine Manila bay is now home to more than 10 thousand pilgrims worldwide seeking for one miracle or other through the holy intercession of Our Lady of Perpetual Help.

On the novena booklet of Our Lady of Perpetual Help, there is another testimony that would interest you, O Christian soul. It was a testimony recorded in the Boston Shrine testimonials. The testimony was about a directress of a college who had a horrible cancer in her breast that had broken out in 3 places. The most distinguished doctors of Boston had examined the disease and adjudged it incurable unless there was a happy outcome to surgical operation. The sick woman, although with repugnance, had to consent to it; but first she began a novena to Our Lady of Perpetual Help. Eight days had passed without attaining the desired result and the operation was to be performed on the following day. Several, distinguished professors, from the university among them its head, were to cooperate in this painful undertaking. They put the sick woman to sleep with a soporific drink and placed her on the operating table. The head surgeon was somewhat distant, and the surgeon assigned to begin that risky task, asked him with which of the three wounds he was to start. "With the largest", he was answered; but behold; the surgeon could not find any cancer. Very courageously the head surgeon approached the sick woman, and imagine his surprise when neither could he find any sign of the terrible disease, nevertheless, he affirmed solemnly to the doctors who were present that previous evening and that very morning himself had seen three horrible cancers in the breast of the sick woman. He added that their disappearance was a mystery to him.

They released the sick woman and awakened her. Not feeling any pain she asked why they had released her. They assured her that the operation was not necessary. Having convinced herself of that fact, she began to give thanks to Our Lady of Perpetual Help, declaring to the incredulous but stunned doctors, that this was the work of the good Mother in whose honor a novena was coming to an end on that very same day. *(Culled from the Novena book in honor of Our Lady of Perpetual Help by Rev. F.J Gaudze, and published by The Franciscan Minims of The Perpetual Help of Mary the House of Atonement)*

O Christian soul, the above miracle was God's wondrous deeds through the holy intercessions of Our Lady of Perpetual Help in Boston US, 1883. It is such a miracle that many unbelievers will look at and ask, 'how is this possible?". Oh, nothing is impossible before God, the creator of the body and the soul. Nothing is impossible before God, the creator of heaven and earth; who calls each stars of the heavens by their names; and my scientific research tells me that there are about 1 billion trillions of stars in the galaxies(Psalm147:4).

Rightly, one thing with miracles is that they are always beyond human comprehension as the fetus in the womb. One thing with miracles is that they are ever renewing as you cannot step your feet in the river having the same experience. In miracles, there is always the "THIRD FORCE" above the ordinary that happens. 1 Corinthians 2:10 says that, "the Spirit of God explores the depth of all things"; the Spirit of God restores and renews all things. And in the previous verse it says, "What no eye has seen and no ear has heard (miracles and favors inclusive), what the mind of man cannot visualize; all that God has prepared for those who love him". Therefore, it is to those who love God and to those WHOM He has blessed with His Spirit to them will be revealed the depth of God's Spirit and the omnipotent works of miracles. It is to such souls that will understand the power of God.

ON A PERSONAL NOTE

Personally, I have witnessed the wonders of this very devotion. I have witnessed the miracles associated with the Holy image of Our Lady of Perpetual Help. Our Lady/Mother of Perpetual Help has been my succor and help. I am not excluding the great friend that is Jesus.

I have had several occasions in which I was stranded and hopeless. I have had situations of near impossibilities, but calling on Our Lady of Perpetual Help to intercede for me before the ***HEAVENLY THRONE*** I found hope, succor and reliefs. One was in 2013 when I lost my mum and my business took a nosedive. I was stranded at that time that no help seemed to come. But I called on Our Lady of Perpetual Help to intercede for me before Jesus, as she is the closest person most conformed to Jesus, just like a son would go through her mother to receive a gift from his father who had been upset about his poor academic growth, a new force dawned on me and the paths to excellence and greatness were shown to me. I began to make progress in life and in business; to a definite purpose of living. The other was in 2018 when my wife was both pregnant and had to undergo another surgical operation after the first appendectomy she had before she became pregnant had caused massive fluids of pus in her left ovarian side. We sought the intercessory and perpetual help of Our Lady of Perpetual Help for a complete-free operation. The operation did not only become successful, the pregnancy stayed till nine successful months and our first daughter was born. These and many more are some of my experiences of the Holy Icon that, Mary is ever ready to assist us in dark moments of impossibilities. According to Fr. William O'Connor, "Go to Our Lady of Perpetual Succor. She will hear you, she will help you, and she will get for you all good".

THE CONNECTIONS

I implore you then O Christian soul, that there are multiple favors you would gain when you turn to Mary asking for her ***perpetual and maternal help***. Mary as I pointed out in my discussion on the Pieta and in this blessed episode of her glorious revelation is ever ready to assist us in whatever condition. Mary is ever ready to assist in us in dark moments of impossibilities as she assented in Luke 1:37. Mary is ever ready to lead us to God crush the head of the enemy. Mary is ever ready to help us swallow up death in victory (1 Corinthians 15:54). Oh, we call this devotion "Perpetual" because Mary till eternity is ever ready to lead us to God. We call this devotion "Perpetual" because in this divine devotion we also find the connecting point between Genesis 3: 23-24 and Luke 23: 42-43; the first was when man was chased out of the paradise, and the second was when on the same cross of Calvary Jesus welcomed the thief on his left-hand side into paradise; and so will He welcome into paradise those who will come to Him in true repentance. These two divine scriptural passages also merged together to give us the "Hodighitria" who is Mary; for at the end of that glorious sacrifice on the cross Jesus finally gave us his Mother as our true maternal source of help. These two connections also re-echoed that eternal message at the beginning of the creation, "that it is not good for man to be alone....let us find him a helper-woman" (Genesis 2:18), and that victorious message at the foot of the cross: "Son, this is your Mother (your Help), Mother, this is your Son (John 19:26-27)". The first was in the beginning of the creation. The second was at the restoration of a new order.

****O Mary, Our Lady of Perpetual help, we pray thee to intercede for us in moments of difficulties and confusions. Intercede for those (mention your name or anyone you know) who are seeking for the fruit of the womb. Intercede for those who are seeking for breakthroughs. Intercede for those who are in distress of my mind and body, like you interceded for the merchant whose ship was about to capsize. Intercede for those who are in the hospitals and those who have no one to care for them. O ancient love of the Father, look unto us with compassion that are in terrible conditions of deaths and evil manipulations of the occult. May we rise again with Jesus as the pelican rises up from the pelican! O ancient Star of the Sea, may we be true to our vocations and purposes. Guide us in the ways that will please Jesus. Pray for Us! Intercede for us! Your eternal beauty is deep. Let your beauty shine on the ugliest parts of our lives like the sun over the deep. We pray, I pray and ask in Jesus name, Amen!

The NOVENA

The Novena to Our Lady of Perpetual Help is a 9 days consecutive novena held in honor of Our Lady of Perpetual Help. It is held weekly all over the world. The feast day of this particular title is held every 27th June annually. In 1899, the first booklet for the novena prayer to Our Lady of perpetual Help was first published in Spain. It was republished in United States, between 1927 and 1935, and was first recited in Saint Alphonsus Church in St. Louis, Missouri. Later, the novena booklet got revised by Irish and Australian Redemptorists in June 1948. It got reprinted in many other copies afterwards. In the Philippines, some of these copies were used from 1950's upward. In Nigeria, this novena is also prayed weekly in more than hundred thousand churches and homes all over Nigeria.

The novena is also held weekly every Wednesday in some parishes. The official booklet of the novena was issued by the Redemptorists, and first published by Jose' Maria Cos y Macho, Bishop of Madrid. The present booklet was co-authored by Rev. Leo James English, C.Ss.R, and Fra Gerard O'Donnell. It is officially in use at the Church of San Alphonsus Ligouri in Rome each week, where the original Icon of Our Lady of Perpetual Help is currently enshrined.

To find the complete novena prayer of this Holy devotion, you can get it from the Church of San Alphonsus Ligouri or visit their online site, or visit any Catholic Church bookshop near you. Presently, there are other copies and versions of the novena booklet to Our Lady of Perpetual Help.

The main contents of the novena booklet/prayer include:

The "Immaculate Mary" Hymn

Introductory prayers, petitions and thanksgiving

Hail Mary

Consecration to Our Lady of perpetual help (done every first Wednesday of the month)

Prayer for the sick

Prayer for the home

Novena prayers

Petitions to Our Lady of Perpetual Help

Divine praises

Tantum Ergo

Act of contrition and preparatory prayers

Ejaculatory prayers for courtship, against temptations, financial helps and other breakthroughs

Et cetera...

Sincerely, I strongly believe in the efficacy of these prayers, especially when said with definiteness of purpose and faith. Faith and definiteness of purpose are the undeniable ingredients of prayers and miracles; even of success. When prayers are mixed with faith, love and purpose, they tend to bring into existence their physical form or equivalent. Mary understood this before she sang the 'Magnificat" in Luke 1:38 when she said, "let it be done to me according to thy word". The word "according" in that sentence represents faith speaking without doubt of its physical manifestation. Elizabeth confirmed this glorious act of faith and definiteness of purpose in Luke 1:45 when she said, "yes, blessed is she _who believed_ that the promise made her by the Lord would be _fulfilled_" (emphasis added). Thus when we approach this blessed devotion of Our Lady of Perpetual Help seeking for Mary's divine perpetual help, we should also pray with faith and definiteness of purpose that that which we seek shall be done unto us according to our faith and according to the Word of God living in us.

I pray that the peace of God which surpasses human understanding shall locate you wherever you need divine help and assistance. You shall be lifted high.

CHAPTER THREE

AN ACT OF CONSECRATION TO MARY OR TOTAL CONSECRATION TO MARY

An Act of consecration to Mary according St. Louis Marie-de Montfort is another powerful Marian devotion that would influence your life. It is another Marian devotion of grace and power.

THE BEGINNING

The beginning of my journey to this act of consecration to Mary started in 1995. I was a junior seminarian studying to become a Catholic Priest at St. Paul's Seminary, Ukpor. Then, I was 14 years old. Then, we had a senior seminarian who taught us piety and deep love for Mary. His name was Mike Akaigwe. Mike Akaigwe, now a Roman Catholic priest, was a charismatic and influential teacher of truth and of the many impartations of elevation. Every night, he would gather us like the hen would gather her chicks to teach us heaven and the interpretations of the scriptures, and of holy and divine call. His constant message was on the unification of our hearts to the Sacred Heart of Jesus through Mary.

Then also, I had no special interest in the things of Mary except to pray the Rosary ordinarily and listen to Mike Akaigwe's peripatetic sermons. The fires in those sermons were like blazing torches. They ignited lots of souls. The fires in those sermons were like burning charcoals. They molded many of us into whom we have become. Many of us grew sprouted wings and deep roots out of the flora and fauna of those fiery sermons.

But honestly, I didn't know much or practice much about Mary then. I didn't glory much in the things of Mary. I prayed the rosary and joined the crusades because I saw others praying and joining. I had no deep regard for the love of this Holy Mother. My deep love for Mary started in earnest when I came over to All Hallows Seminary, Onitsha, to complete my SSCE in my SS 3 class. That time, I was a no-nonsense footballer, full of ego and pride until the spirit arrested me one day through Cosmas Uzoukwu (FR) and Mike Udo.

Cosmas and Mike were two great friends of mine. They brought me closer to Mary. They were the darts like Elijah's mantle on Elisha that fell off from Mike Akaigwe's sacerdotal ephod and began to blossom. Like Akaigwe, Cosmas and Mike urged me to come to Christ and concentrate my life deeply on Jesus through Mary. I obeyed their words and came to Jesus through Mary, just like a child would go through his mother to get the attention of his father. Thus sometime around March, 1999, I had my total consecration to Jesus through Mary according to St. Louis Marie de Montfort. After my consecration, I saw a great light like the people of Zebulum and Naphtali. My life changed. My inner life became new. I began to do things ordinarily I wouldn't have done, with power and great composure. I saw new meanings to the essence of life and its vicissitudes. I saw new meanings to life of holiness and greatness. I designed my life then in a way that it was programmed for life of prayer and excellence. I lived each day with purpose and desire for impartation.

Sincerely, all these happened in my life because I came to know Jesus more through his Mother. Mary led me to Jesus in such a way that defied months of studies and reflections as she had hastened the miracles at Cana in Galilee. Mary is our salvation catalyst. She hastens things for us. Oh then, I would sit on a long pew in our Chapel besides the Sanctuary opposite the sacristy gazing on Jesus through Mary for a long time. My sermon one day on the essence of living a godly life became so touching that Kingsley Ogujawa, may His Soul rest in peace, approached me and said "wonderful my dear, keep it up!". All these are to tell you, O Christian soul, love of the Father, that when a soul is truly consecrated to Jesus through Mary many things begin to happen. Many things which hitherto might look ordinary would begin to take shape and form in an extraordinary way. This also is the sole meaning of the word "incarnation".

A SPECIAL WAY OF CONSECRATION

Dear beloved of the Father! The consecration to Mary is a special way of uniting our souls and being to Mary. It is a special way of uniting our hearts and being in love with Jesus through Mary, who is also the mother of God. In life, two things make us more divine than human. One is the soul; the other is the spirit. The soul is the seat of power, understanding and love. The spirit is the "movement, the force behind every momentum and influence. Thus when we consecrate our spirit, soul and body to Jesus through Mary, we replicate in all honesty that we want to garner the graces, the power, the influence that were bestowed on Mary, the mother of Jesus. We replicate in all honesty that we want to be like Jesus with the help of his mother; for if our consecration to Mary do not lead us to Jesus, then it is useless. We also replicate that we want Mary to guide our steps and intercede for us in all things, for she will never allow our souls to perish.

In John 19: 25-27, something happened that showed us Mary will never allow our souls perish when we consecrate our souls to Jesus through her, and why also she is our Mother extraordinaire.

It was at the crucifixion of Christ. Peter had denied Jesus 3 times and ran away. He was nowhere to be seen when the Master whom he had been with for 3 years was crucified on the cross. Each of the times Peter denied Jesus signified literally the number of years he had been with the Master. The apostles, both those who were seen at the fig tree and those whose daughters and servants he healed, had all deserted their master and ran away. None except John was seen at the foot of the cross. Judas Iscariot, the previous night, had denied and betrayed Jesus. He told the Chief priests that "him I shall kiss is the one". His kiss was the 'ripper knife' like Brutus' upon Caesar.

But in all these, Mary, the mother of the Redeemer and the Redeemed, stood by his son **_till the end_** (emphasis marked). All her prayerful intentions were to witness the glorious seeds of this divine transformation. Mary was the big influence that made John to remain resolute and stay before the cross. John might have seen her at the foot of the cross and said in his heart, "Oh, the mother of my Savior! If she could remain so strong, why shouldn't I?" Mary was the encouragement and the fortitude for John to stay at the cross. No wonder, Jesus on looking down from the ancient cross saw John and His mother Mary. His heart was so pleased to see His mother and the one he beloved. Imagine yourself at that critical moment to see your mother and a student friend when all had deserted you. _Wouldn't you also be pleased for her to glory in your victory_? Thus immediately Jesus saw his mother and the apostle he beloved, He commanded John to take Mary home; that very heart, who has conformed so much to his pains and has **_remained so strong in his victory_ _(emphasis marked)_**. He also told Mary implicitly in return, never to leave whosoever comes to her for help and protection. John represented us in that very command, and the word "home" in his command to John (us) signifies two things: for John to take Mary home as a special mother and for Mary **_look after him as a special mother_**. All was centered on Mary and in Mary. The word 'home' also means both spiritual and physical homes where Jesus together with His mother will reign in our hearts and homes that God be praised at all times. These, dear Christian soul, are other obvious revelations to the consecration of our souls to Jesus through Mary. These, dear Christian soul, are obvious revelations why Mary will never allow our souls to perish when we hide ourselves under her maternal protection.

Hence, when we consecrate our souls to Jesus through Mary, we implore Mary to lead us home in her maternal care amidst the thorns and thistles that push us away from the kingdom of God. We say in our Igbo culture, "that when a man is ostracized from his fatherland, he is always welcomed in his motherland". Mary welcomes us when we deviate from the true path that is Jesus. She leads us back to the Savior in such a way a mother would lead her wards home. She prays for us. She intercedes on our behalf. Like the true mother she is, she bears our pains and joys.

THE TOTAL CONSECRATION TO MARY

In 1712, 4 years before his death in 1716, St. Louis Marie de-Montfort formulated a complete way through which we consecrate our hearts and souls to Jesus through Mary. He called it an act of consecration; total consecration to Jesus through Mary. In St. Louis Marie de- Montfort's views, since God deemed it fit to save us through Mary; He will also hear us through Mary. In St. Louis de-Montfort's view, it was through Blessed Mary that Jesus came into the world, it is also through her that He must reign in the world; that since Jesus came into the world through Mary and for us to be close to Jesus we should go through Mary; that of all creature the one most conformed to Jesus Christ is Mary. It follows that among all devotions that which most consecrates and conforms a soul to our Lord is devotion to Mary, His Holy mother, and that the more a soul is consecrated to her the more will it be consecrated to Jesus Christ.

Numerous Popes, Venerable, and Bishops were influenced by St. Louis Marie de Montfort's teachings and inspirational writings. They practiced this devotion to the truth and were influenced by its impacts. Among them was St. John Paul II.

The total consecration to Jesus through Mary is thus a perfect way of consecrating our soul, spirit and body to Jesus through Mary. It is a 33-day program, starting with a 12-day preparatory period in which a soul intending to be consecrated is nurtured and prepared for the actual consecration.

The total consecration to Jesus through Mary is divided into two parts: 12 days of preparation and 3 consecutive weeks of total concentration to Mary. The 3 consecutive weeks, together with the 12-day preparatory period, make it 33 days in total;

the 34th day being the actual day of the consecration on any Marian feast of your choice.

THE 12 DAYS OF PREPARATION

On the first day of the preparation, the soul preparing to be consecrated is taught the value of emptying oneself of the spirit of the world, obedience to the word of God and freeing oneself from the concupiscence of the flesh. The scriptural verse upon which the foundation of this first day of preparation is laid is Matthew 5:1-9. Here, Jesus teaches us the "Eight Beatitudes". He admonishes us to imbibe the spirit of humility, meekness, mercy, purity, hunger and thirst for righteousness, and the desire to be called the children of God for we are the salt and light of the world. This first day of preparation, like other days as well, follows a prayerful sequence that starts with innovation to the Trinity and ends with Marian hymns.

On the second day of the preparation, the soul preparing to be consecrated to JESUS through Mary is taught the vanity of all things with emphasis on Praying in secret, giving alms in secret, and on the secrets of Our Lord's prayer. The scriptural passage here is Matthew 5:48, 6:1-5.

The third day, the fourth day, the fifth day, the sixth day, the seventh day, the eighth day, the ninth day, the tenth day, the eleventh day and the twelfth day of the preparatory period, have their respective messages and reflections on justice, effective prayer, life of holiness and chastity, and total submission to God with biblical and scriptural emphasis from "The Imitation of Christ" by Thomas A'Kempis. These make up the 12-day preparatory period in which a soul intending to be consecrated must pass through before he or she is allowed passage into the next phase of the consecration.

The next phase of the consecration is the remaining 3 CONSECUTIVE WEEKS of total consecration.

THE FIRST WEEK

Here in the first week, a soul willing to be consecrated goes through a rigorous process of soul searching and character formation. He or she is taught the value of obtaining _self-knowledge_ through the light of Christ and at the feet of Mary. He or she is equally admitted into the consciousness that to 'live is Jesus; to die is Jesus through Mary'. The conformity of these two hearts are expressed in such a way that the intending soul for consecration sees herself or himself as only an instrument in the hands of God.

THE SECOND WEEK

The second week of the total consecration is a week on the Blessed Virgin Mary. The week carries in its full regalia the 10 principal virtues of Mary: humility, lively faith, blind obedience, continual mental prayer, mortification in all things, purity, ardent charity, patience, angelic sweetness and divine wisdom. The soul is taught these great virtues that he or she might approach or come to Christ fully through Mary. These great virtues help the soul to obtain full knowledge of Mary, that in understanding these virtues of the Blessed Virgin Mary he or she might learn how to please God in all things.

THE THIRD WEEK

The third week of the total consecration is the final week of the total consecration before the final day of the consecration. In this week, a soul about to be consecrated is finally drawn before Jesus Christ, the Alpha and Omega. In coming before Christ, the intending soul for consecration is taught the knowledge of Christ that he or she might obtain a full knowledge of Him who had conquered sin and death and has given us full victory in God. Christ is presented before the intending soul as the final revelation of God. He is presented before the intending soul as the giver of life and Lord of all things, who is the head of all principalities (Colossians 2:10). The intending soul is thus enlightened to imitate Christ in all things, that in imitating Christ in all things he or she shall never walk in darkness. This is a special week of consecration and blessings. This is a special week of love and appreciation, where the soul is saturated with deep love for Christ through Mary.

These, O Christian Soul, are the complete steps, thirty three days in all, that a soul partakes in before he or she is finally consecrated to Jesus through Mary on the final day of the consecration.

THE FINAL DAY OF THE CONSECRATION

On the final day of the consecration, the consecrated soul comes to the altar before a priest to make his vow or her final commitment to the heart of Jesus through Mary. He or she is given an Act of total consecration prayer to pray and sign his or her name at the end of this prayer. The act of total consecration prayer contains the vows of this holy devotion. In this holy vow, the consecrated SOUL vows to reject Satan, his pomp and works forever; that he or she will give himself or herself entirely to Christ and carry his or her cross in life along with Christ; that he or she will also honor the Blessed Virgin Mary and obey God in all things. The consecrated soul is to renew this vow with the act of total consecration prayer every year on the date he or she made this vow and signed it.

AFTER THE TOTAL CONSECRATION

After the total consecration, the consecrated soul chooses a particular act of physical commitment out of the 4 physical commitments proposed by St. Louis Marie de Montfort. This is for the consecrated soul to show his or her outward commitment to this holy devotion. It is also a sign that he or she is now "a holy slave to Mary" in his love or her love for Jesus. In his exemplary life, St. Louis Marie de Montfort wore chains on his arms and feet to mark this commitment and as a token of his dedication and love for Mary. As such, he proposed that all who should honor Mary in this holy regard should also wear a little chain to confess this holy commitment. He proposed wearing several smallish chain links with no clasp, or a special large chain link bracelet, or a thick chain link with a Miraculous Medal, or the consecrated soul wears any Marian medal associated with the feast of the consecration. In my own case, we were given brown scapulars according to St. Simon Stock to wear. This became my own act of physical commitment to this holy vow to love Jesus all the days of my life and to also honor his mother.

BENEFITS OF THIS HOLY CONSECRATION

Oh Christian soul! The Total Consecration to Mary is a powerful Marian devotion. It purifies the heart and makes it ever ready for salvation in Christ Jesus. It strengthens the will in its quest to abstain from sin. It renders grace and power to the soul. It makes us efficient in serving God and denying ourselves from the concupiscence of the flesh. It reminds us the futility of all things and the glory that is in Jesus through Mary.

To find the complete manual of the Total Consecration to Jesus through Mary, you can find it on any Catholic bookshop online or offline. You can read the True devotion to Mary by St .Louis Marie de Montfort.

Excerpts from the Act of Total Consecration Prayer

ACT OF CONSECRATION PRAYER:

Total Consecration to Jesus through Mary

By St. Louis de Montfort

O ETERNAL and incarnate Wisdom! O sweetest and most adorable Jesus! True God and true man, only

Son of the Eternal Father, and of Mary, always virgin! I adore Thee profoundly in the bosom and splendors of Thy Father during eternity; and I adore Thee also in the virginal bosom of Mary, Thy most worthy Mother, in the time of Thine incarnation.

I give Thee thanks for that Thou hast annihilated Thyself, taking the form of a slave in order to rescue me from the cruel slavery of the devil. I praise and glorify Thee for that Thou hast been pleased to submit Thyself to Mary, Thy holy Mother, in all things, in order to make me Thy faithful slave through her.

But, alas! Ungrateful and faithless as I have been, I have not kept the promises which I made so solemnly to Thee in my Baptism; I have not fulfilled my obligations; I do not deserve to be called Thy child, nor yet Thy slave; and as there is nothing in me which does not merit Thine anger and Thy repulse, I dare not come by myself before Thy most holy and august Majesty.

It is on this account that I have recourse to the intercession of Thy most holy Mother, whom Thou hast given me for a mediatrix with Thee. It is through her that I hope to obtain of Thee contrition, the pardon of my sins, and the acquisition and preservation of wisdom.

Hail, then, O immaculate Mary, living tabernacle of the Divinity, where the Eternal Wisdom willed to be hidden and to be adored by angels and by men! Hail, O Queen of Heaven and earth, to whose empire everything is subject which is under God. Hail, O sure refuge of sinners, whose mercy fails no one. Hear the desires which I have of the Divine Wisdom; and for that end receive the vows and offerings which in my lowliness I present to thee.

I, _____________________, a faithless sinner, renew and ratify today in thy hands the vows of my Baptism; I renounce forever Satan, his pomps and works; and I give myself entirely to Jesus Christ, the Incarnate Wisdom, to carry my cross after Him all the days of my life, and to be more faithful to Him than I have ever been before.

In the presence of all the heavenly court I choose thee this day for my Mother and Mistress. I deliver and consecrate to thee, as thy slave, my body and soul, my goods, both interior and exterior, and even the value of all my good actions, past, present and future; leaving to thee the entire and full right of disposing of me, and all that belongs to me, without exception, according to thy good pleasure, for the greater glory of God in time and in eternity.

Receive, O benignant Virgin, this little offering of my slavery, in honor of, and in union with, that subjection which the Eternal Wisdom deigned to have to thy maternity; in homage to the power which both of you have over this poor sinner, and in thanksgiving for the privileges with which the Holy Trinity has favored thee. I declare that I wish henceforth, as thy true slave, to seek thy honor and to obey thee in all things.

O admirable Mother, present me to thy dear Son as His eternal slave, so that as He has redeemed me by thee, by thee He may receive me! O Mother of mercy, grant me the grace to obtain the true Wisdom of God; and for that end receive me among those whom thou lovest and teachest, whom thou leadest, nourishest and protectest as thy children and thy slaves.

O faithful Virgin, make me in all things so perfect a disciple, imitator and slave of the Incarnate Wisdom, Jesus Christ thy Son, that I may attain, by thine intercession and by thine example, to the fullness of His age on earth and of His glory in Heaven. Amen

----

Sign your name here

Date

IN CONCLUSION

FINDING YOUR INNER WAY TO JESUS THROUGH MARY

Like I said in the preface of this book, Mary is a deep revelation by God. This is because when the Scripture says in Ephesians 1:4 "that God choose us in Christ even before the foundation of the world", this scriptural passage also points to the fact that God who choose us in Christ Jesus had also this eternal beauty called Mary in mind; for when God chose us in Christ He also chose the very 'means' of this total salvation. Suffice it to say here O Christian soul that the Marian devotions which I have enumerated above are not all there are to Marian devotions. There are several other Marian devotions. The Total Consecration to Jesus through Mary is just one of these devotions. The devotion to Our Lady of Perpetual Help is another. The Holy Rosary is yet another. Significantly, what these holy devotions have in common is that they lead us closer to Jesus through Mary. They present Mary to us as our Maternal Help and great Intercessor.

Therefore, O Christian soul, I thank you for going through these glorious episodes with me. May God bless you abundantly! I thank you for meditating with me on this excellent masterpiece. May the fountain of your life never run dry! I urge you then, as I would urge all who comes to me, to choose any Marian devotion of your choice or the three I discussed above, while considering also other Marian devotions, to pray and activate actively in your life. Have it in your subconscious mind that Mary is your "Hodighitria"; Mary is a deep revelation by God. She is the Star of the Sea. She is the mother of God. She is our help in times of troubles.

In the events that took place before the birth of John the Baptist in Luke 1:39-45, something happened that should draw your attention. When Mary heard that Elizabeth was six months pregnant, she left all she was doing and journeyed to a far distant land to stay with Elizabeth. Mary did not consider that she was also carrying the Messiah, as most of us would behave to think. She did not consider that she was filled with the power of the Most High God; therefore Elizabeth should come to her first as the new Sheriff in town. All her humble thoughts were to help her kinswoman who was in dire need of mutual affection; for Elizabeth's miraculous condition would have caused many to question her pregnancy and flee from her. Thus, what happened immediately Mary stepped her feet inside Elizabeth's house is what I want you to briefly mediate and ponder upon.

Immediately Elizabeth saw Mary and heard her greetings, the child in her womb leapt in joy. Elizabeth was filled with the Holy Ghost, and greeted Mary in return saying, "..... Who am I, that the mother of my Redeemer should visit me"? Please, pause over this. Elizabeth did not know Mary as the mother of God before now. She only knew her as her relative; the daughter of Joachim and Anne. Thus in Elizabeth's greeting, there was a strange order of divine communication; what has not been seen about Christ Jesus became the order of what was talked about and seen by Elizabeth.

Ordinarily Elizabeth wouldn't have made that bold confession like Peter did in Mathew 16:16, but being filled with the Holy Ghost who overshadowed her immediately Mary stepped her feet in her presence, she was able to make that solid confession. She saw in Mary the Trinity. She saw in Mary: God the Father, the creator, God the Son, the Redeemer, and God the Spirit, the Comforter. Her little baby also leapt in thunderous confirmation to this glorious manifestation. How can an unborn baby not make such euphoria of joy when it feels the presence of its source of life and strength?

Remember then, O Christian soul, the type of joy you would feel when you consecrate your being to Jesus through Mary. Mary will activate your spirit as she activated Elizabeth's. She is full of the Holy Ghost (Luke 1:35). She will cause your spirit to overflow with joy and happiness as you come to the revelation and knowledge of her son, Jesus Christ. Therefore, it is with this joy and happiness that I conclude the remaining chapter of this book with you praying:

O Mary, full of the Holy Ghost and grace, come to our aids that are in need of your grace. Let us leap in joy like John and rejoice in jubilation like the granddaughter of Zion. Help us in our difficult moments. Pray for us. Intercede for us against witches and wizards. May we garner the graces that were bestowed on you. May we be ever ready to assist others who are also in need of love and compassion, that in doing so our love and compassion for others will also be replicated in your outward and maternal love for us. Teach us to love Jesus, and make us always bear in mind that we have a heavenly place to go, where God will be all in all and where all our heart desires will be granted in Jesus name. Amen!

Thank you Mother Millennial....

PART 2

12 VICTORIOUS PSALMS OF HEALING AND EMPOWERMENT

For you, O Christian soul that started this journey with us, we stated at the beginning of this book that we shall present to you "12 Victorious Psalms of Healing and Empowerment". We made it clear that it is also going to be among the geographical portion of this book. Our promise has not waned; only that this book would not reflect how we would like to present these 12 Victorious Psalms to you in full dimension. The 12 Victorious Psalms are: Psalm 1, Psalm 2, Psalm 16, Psalm 19, Psalm 23, Psalm 24, Psalm 46, Psalm 51, Psalm 68, Psalm 90, Psalm 91, and Psalm 149. We implore you to get our second book on these, titled *"**12 Victorious Psalms of Healing and Empowerment'**.* There, you will understand the power of Psalms. There, your inner eyes will be opened to the understanding of divine precepts and commands with powerful prayer points and paraphrases.

The book of Psalms is actually one book that has changed many lives. I remember in year 2002 when I was psychological disturbed and how having prayed Psalm 25 daily, I was relieved of the spirit of confusion which had deprived my joy in the Lord. I was joyful at that time that no word could quantify my joy and happiness.

The book of Psalms is also a book of praises and blessings that has lived for ages. The ancient laid powerful credence to this auspicious book of prayers and testimonies. They used this book in asserting divine will and in wonderful admonitions.

In Acts of the Apostles 2:26-27, Peter told all who were gathered about the Pentecost how the Psalmist in Psalm 16 vs.9-10 had prophesied that the Holy One would never see corruption. The Psalmist prophesied the resurrection of Jesus and the power of his resurrection. Peter told those who gathered on that day how this prophecy has been fulfilled. Remember that Peter had just received the Holy Ghost and his eyes had been opened to the revelations of the words of the Psalmist. What he said were not just mere biblical contexts; they were revealed to him by the Spirit. Peter also quoted Psalm 2 in Acts 4:25-26, speaking of the futility of men, and of the wonders and miracles God performs in the lives of his people.

Psalm 68:1 has more than 12 instances in the book of Psalms where God was prayed to ARISE and defend his people.

In Acts 1:20, the apostles chose Mathias to take the place of Judas Iscariot based on what the Psalmist said in Psalm 109: 4-8: "His Position, let another take".

Apostle Paul quoted Psalm 2:7 in Acts 13: 34 to tell of the victory we have in Christ Jesus. He also quoted Psalm 16 vs. 9-10 like Peter in that same chapter.

In Luke 4:10, the devil himself quoted Psalm 91:11 to tell you the efficacy of Psalms and the ministerial powers of angels.

Christ also quoted Psalm 118:22-23 in Mathew 21:42 about the stone the builders rejected which has become the cornerstone. He talked about himself in this plain text, which Peter after healing the crippled man at the Beautiful Gate told the elders and scribes in Acts 4:10-11 that Christ was the Chief cornerstone of that healing and restoration.

In Hebrews 1:1-14, the writer cited Psalm 110 in revealing Christ as the final revelation of God. The writer quoted Psalm 2:7 to reveal the kingship of Christ Jesus and His divine authority over all things.

Therefore, there are many instances, O Christian soul, of the glorious use of the book of Psalms. There are many testimonies and accreditations associated with this book of divine miracles. Many have prayed their way out using this book of ageless wisdom and psalms. Thus in the "12 Victorious Psalms of Healing and Empowerment", I made conscientious efforts to reveal the divine powers and moral teachings inherent in these Psalms. Other remaining 138 Psalms are also powerful with their specific divine insights, hymns, prayer points and admonitions. I chose these 12 Psalms for us to reflect upon, with their specific prayers, based on my own experiences of these Psalms, and how these Psalms had worked wonders in the lives of those who prayed them assiduously and religiously. I have no doubt that when you pray these Psalms, sing the hymns of these Psalms and meditate passionately on them, that which you seek for shall be granted to you in Jesus name, Amen!

There is power in Psalms and in the _effective repetitions_ of the words of the Psalmists. Do not doubt the effects of prayers or listen to what the world and the devil say. There is power in Psalms.

WANT TO REACH US?

We run the Joppa Family Outreach. We spread the gospel of Christ through evangelism, hospital visitations, and youth/educational empowerment. You can reach us for your retreats, testimonies, prayer requests et cetera via e-mail at admin@joppafamily.org, call us on +2348110840272 or visit our website at www.joppafamily.org

At Joppa family we also publish articles, newsletters and other works of impacts and dominion. You can become part of our sponsors by reaching us on +2348110840272.

Finally, if this book of prayers and blessings has impacted your soul heavily, please help us to spread this work of divine glory.

Nebo Peter Chinedu is the author of "12 Victorious Psalms of Healing and Empowerment", "The Virgin Most Powerful: 3 Powerful Marian Devotions That Will Change your Life", and the convener of Joppa Family Outreach.

References:

1. True devotion to Mary: St. Louis Marie de Montfort
2. Novena book in honor of Our Lady of Perpetual Help: Rev. F.J Gaudze, and published by The Franciscan Minims of The Perpetual Help of Mary the House of Atonement
3. The Jerusalem Bible
4. Ben Hur: A tale of Christ: General Lew Wallace
5. Catholic.org
6. Monasteryicons.com
7. The Life of Christ: Fulton J. Sheen
8. Redemptoris Mater
9. Rosarium Virginis Mariae
10. Treatise on the True devotion to the Blessed Virgin, St. Louis de Montfort